The Smart Writing Handbook

Laura Robb

DEDICATED TO TEACHERS™

DEDICATED TO TEACHERS™

An imprint of Heinemann
Heinemann
361 Hanover Street
Portsmouth, NH 03801–3912
www.heinemann.com

Offices and agents throughout the world

"Dedicated to Teachers" is a trademark of Greenwood Publishing Group, Inc.

Editor: Tina Miller
Design and Production: Palmer Creative Group
Text illustration: Jim Espey

Library of Congress Cataloging-in-Publication Data
CIP data is on file with the Library of Congress

ISBN-13: 978-0-325-04371-5
ISBN-10: 0-325-04371-X

Printed in the United States of America

16 15 14 13 12 VP 1 2 3 4 5

Dear Student,

"We just want the freedom to write," say the middle school students I know. You are tired of rules and guidelines, lessons at the teacher's pace rather than your own. I couldn't agree more. This handbook encourages that freedom by emphasizing the importance of choosing a topic for in-school writing that you care deeply about. But it also offers tips, rules, and guidelines that enable you to communicate your ideas, your thoughts and feelings, and your research to others.

Writing is an important part of your everyday life. I know many of you write outside of school—and love it! You send text messages; you email, blog, and instant message with friends; and you write fan fiction. Writing is also an important part of middle school English and content classes. I hope this handbook will help you with any kind of writing you engage in, both at school and at home.

So that the handbook responds to your needs, I asked two seventh-grade students to read it and offer me feedback: Maggie Gildea, who lives in Auburn, New Hampshire, and Keaton Leta, who lives in Berryville, Virginia. You'll find their quotes throughout the handbook.

I hope this handbook helps you find joy in writing and communicating with others, and offers tips and models that you will find useful as you plan, draft, revise, and edit.

Sincerely,

Laura Robb

Laura Robb

Dedication

For Maggie Gildea and Keaton Leta, with deep appreciation for all your work and help.

Contents

Heinemann Website for Students

Heinemann has created a website especially for you:
www.smartwritinghandbook.com
Visit the website to view or download these materials:

* Handouts that can help you with different writing genres

* Sample criteria that are developed for specific writing genres

* Mentor texts that give examples of strong writing

* Writing plan forms you can use and review

* Peer- and self-evaluation forms that you and your at-home writing partner can complete

Developing At-Home Writing Partnerships

At school, you work by partnering up with a classmate. Tapping into a classmate's expertise makes the writing as much fun as spending the day at your favorite theme park—well, almost as much fun!

Since I believe that writing partnerships are so helpful, I'm encouraging you to have one or two partners you can turn to when completing writing assignments at home. At home, you can *talk* to your writing partner by texting, instant messaging, or emailing. You might even use your cell phone to call and talk about your writing. An at-home partner can give you the support you need for school writing assignments.

Buried Treasure

Having at-home writing partnerships is like finding buried treasure: no money, no priceless jewels, but lots of feedback and support to help make the writing great.

Here are six ways an at-home writing partner can support you:

1. Listen. Your partner will listen as you talk to find a topic, figure out a plot or argument, or explain why this task bores you. As you talk, you often solve the writing problem.

2. Discuss. Exchanging ideas with your partner gives both of you the chance to think about and advise each other on titles, writing plans, characters' personality traits, leads, and endings.

3. Read. It's easy to attach part of your draft or the entire draft to an email and then talk about your questions with your partner. If you don't have a home computer, use a computer in your local public library.

4. Get Feedback. Ask your partner for feedback on a lead, an ending, or a verb, or ask whether you should tell or show. Share any question you have about your writing with your partner. Jot notes as you talk so you recall your partner's advice.

5. Revise. Think about the feedback your partner offered. Choose what *you* feel works, and use the input to revise parts of your writing.

6. Edit. A peer partner can make editing, which can feel like a chore you want to avoid, quite pleasant. Your partner's x-ray editing vision will pick up punctuation, spelling, and grammar problems that you don't see.

Starting an At-Home Writer's Notebook

"When I think about writing topics, I often think about memories or people I will never forget."
MAGGIE G., GRADE 7

Did you know that most writers keep notebooks? Writers do this so they can easily recall an idea. Unless I write them down, the thoughts I had in the morning are gone by the evening. If your cell phone has a "notebook app," that's a great place to jot ideas. You can also create a writer's notebook on your home computer.

Why Keep a Notebook at Home?

Writing ideas! Writing ideas! Writing ideas! Keeping a writer's notebook at home trains your eye to look deeply and your ear to listen carefully—that gives you ideas. Smells, tastes, and touch fire your imagination and more ideas flow. Keeping a writer's notebook on your home computer allows you to access and use your ideas on the computer in your classroom.

At night, I keep a pad and pencil near my bed and jot down an idea if I wake up with one worth remembering. Then I transfer these jots to my online notebook to keep everything in one place. What's weird about this strategy is that sometimes a dream or a thought that wakes me up is already in my online notebook.

One night I dreamt that I floated down a waterfall, my grandmother with me; she was pale and ghostly looking. I jotted on my pad—"floated down waterfall, grandmother with me, she looks pale and ghostly"—and went back to sleep. Later that day, I entered my notes into my online journal and noticed something I had already written: "letter came, grandmother very ill, need to see her, will travel on weekend, remembering the stories she told, the treats in her pocketbook." The similarity

between my dream and my online entry caused me to drive three hundred miles to see my grandmother; I was able to spend time with her the day before she died.

You're wondering, so what's the big message here? Well, without my online notebook, I might not make or see connections. Why? Most of the time, I forget my dreams and what I wanted to jot down.

Now check out the suggestions for collecting ideas for your online notebook in the box on page 9. Try them. Add your own ideas; note them on a sticky note that you tape to the list in the handbook. Exchange your new ideas with your writing partner. The point is to collect dozens of ideas in your online notebook. This gives you the choices that can lead you to the writing topic you're truly passionate about.

15 Tips for Collecting Ideas in Your Online Notebook

1. Surf the Internet to see if an idea springs to mind.

2. Read the titles of books for ideas.

3. Make a list of what you did that day.

4. Make a list of three to four feelings you had during a day, and relate the feelings to the event or person who caused them.

5. Describe an event you witnessed.

6. Record a dream or a fantasy.

7. Look outside a window in your house, and describe what you see and feel.

8. Read newspaper headings.

9. Listen to others talk when you're in the school cafeteria or locker room.

10. Close your eyes and hear the sounds surrounding you.

11. Relive an experience or a conversation.

12. Think about and describe your favorite person or pet.

13. Describe something unexpected that happened.

14. Explain why you got into trouble.

15. Write about a memory that popped into your mind.

Dip into Entries from Middle School Students' Online Notebooks

Reading the students' entries in the box on page 11 shows you that there is no right or wrong way to use an online notebook. Write in your at-home notebook any ideas, thoughts, groups of words, or lists that you believe have meaning to you and could help you find topics for writing.

Write what's on your mind and in your heart. In your at-home journal, you can be honest and share only what you choose to share with others. Note that students don't always include punctuation. That's okay in your notebook because the point is to jot and remember ideas you might use for a writing assignment.

A Sampling of Entries from Online Notebooks

"The big three are gossiping about me Heard them in the bathroom—they didn't know I was in a stall didn't come out till they left They say that I'm boring cause I study and do my work I hate them I'll never be part of their group Do I want to be What would life be like if I was" **GRADE 7**

"Cleaned my room. Had ants eating pizza crusts I tossed under my bed. Mom is mad. I'm still grounded. She found dirty socks and gym clothes. "Your room stinks," she yelled. I had to do my laundry and wash the floor with disinfectant stuff to "learn a lesson." I don't mind ants and smelly clothes. Why does she?" **GRADE 6**

"Flew my dragon kite at the beach—wind powerful—my mind free. Only think about keep the kite high up and flying. Felt like I was in another universe." **GRADE 7**

"sounds in woods behind my house—cardinal, woodpecker tap-tap-tap-ing, two does, stop, when they see me—hear crunch leaves as they run away" **GRADE 8**

"Scared, timid, unsure." How I felt first day in new school in eighth grade. Would I make friends? Would they let me in? Would I be happy, miserable?" **GRADE 8**

Finding Topics for Writing

"A heart-shaped map helps me decide on a writing topic. Make a large heart and fill it with the things that are important to you—the center being the most important and the edges less important or maybe even something you hate."

MAGGIE G., GRADE 7

Heart map concept invented by Georgia Heard, poet and writing teacher

The key point to remember when searching for a topic is *to choose one you truly care about,* one you will love spending several weeks with as you move through the process of brainstorming, planning, setting criteria, drafting, revising, and editing. If you aren't passionate about a topic, the weeks of writing can feel like forever.

Finding Topics for Narrative Writing

A narrative tells a story and is usually organized in time order. Memoirs and short, short stories are two kinds of narratives you may have written. The skills you have gained at school can help you find topics for your own narratives: a poem, a play, a fantasy, a sci-fi story, or and an historical fiction story or poem.

To find topics for writing narratives:

⁂ Skim and read parts of your writer's notebook.

⁂ Recall a memory, experience, adventure, fantasy, or dream that could become a short, short story or a memoir.

⁂ Talk about your thoughts with a partner.

⁂ Write a list of possible topics on notebook paper.

⁂ Reread the list and add extra ideas that pop into your mind.

⁂ Share your topics with the class as your teacher jots students' ideas on chart paper, and reread the shared list of topics on chart paper to see if these spark new ideas.

⁂ Note new ideas on your list.

Try some of these strategies at home, too!

More suggestions for finding narrative topics

Sometimes after skimming your writer's notebook, talking to your partner, and reading the shared list, a topic you care about still doesn't appear. Try a few of the suggestions that follow to help you find that top-notch topic:

* ❊ Text message two to three possible topic choices to your at-home partner, and ask what he or she thinks of them and if these bring to mind more ideas.

* ❊ Read book titles in the young adult section or a section that interests you at your school or at your community library because titles can spark writing topics.

* ❊ Ask your parents, a brother or sister, or other relatives to tell you about memories they have about you—memories that could turn into a memoir or a short, short story.

* ❊ Go on your class blog and/or school website to read book reviews that others have posted as these might suggest an idea.

* ❊ Skim newspapers and magazines; read their headlines and headings as well as study their photographs and captions to see if ideas develop.

Finding Topics for Argument Writing

Persuasive and analytical essays are two forms of argument you may have practiced. Persuasive essays aim to convince your reader to agree with you; they depend on your experience, viewpoint, and some research. Analytical essays grow out of your ideas about a short story or novel you read.

PERSUASIVE WRITING Types of persuasive writing include writing a newspaper editorial, blogging to persuade, writing an op-ed (opinion editorial), presenting an argument in a letter to the editor of a school or local newspaper, and writing a persuasive speech.

To find topics for persuading others, you may:

* ❊ Recall situations when you convinced your parents to give you your way.

* ❊ Talk to a partner about school issues.

* ❊ Talk to a partner about gaining privileges at school and at home.

* ❊ Write ideas on a piece of notebook paper.

* ❊ Share topic ideas while your teacher writes these on chart paper, and then reread the topics list to see if it gives you other ideas.

More suggestions for persuasive writing

* ❊ Surf approved blog sites on the Internet.

* ❊ Skim a local or national newspaper.

* ❊ Read headlines online from ABC News, MSNBC News, or CNN News.

* ❊ Skim magazines to find issues worthy of argument.

ANALYTICAL WRITING   Types of analytical writing include comparing the themes of two poems; comparing themes, characters, or conflicts in two different short stories or novels; and analyzing setting or characters' decisions in a play.

To find topics for writing an analytical essay:

* Find a short story or novel to analyze. (Your teacher can choose the text, or your teacher can ask you to choose a text.)

* Develop a thesis statement about a theme that was in a story (such as growing up) or key events that helped a character change.

* Work with a partner to find a topic that takes a position, like the examples that follow:
    - Moving to a new city is stressful.
    - Without trust and support, friendships dissolve.
    - Loneliness is painful.

More suggestions for analytical writing

* Read your classmates' analytical essays for other ideas.

* Collaborate with a partner to write an analytical essay on a class wiki, and invite classmates to comment and suggest edits.

Finding Topics for Explanatory Writing

Informative essays and compare/contrast essays involve explanatory writing. The purpose of an informative essay is to present information. The purpose of a compare/contrast essay is to tell how two things are alike and different: for example, two movies or two different accounts of a historical event.

INFORMATIVE ESSAYS Studying informative essays can help you write a newspaper or magazine article, a photo essay, a letter, a blog, a how-to or procedural piece, a book or movie review, and a cause-and-effect essay.

To find topics for an informative essay:

❋ Skim your writer's notebook.

❋ Skim history and science textbooks.

❋ Choose a topic you're an expert on and truly enjoy.

❋ Tap into a hobby you love.

❋ Talk to a partner.

❋ Write possible topics on notebook paper and share these with the class while your teacher records them on chart paper; then reread the list of possible topics to see if these spark new ideas in your mind.

More suggestions for informative essays

* Skim articles in your favorite magazine.

* Read blogs on topics that appeal to you.

* Research an interesting hobby or topic on the Internet to develop an angle and learn new information.

* Watch a documentary video on a topic you love.

COMPARE/CONTRAST ESSAYS The compare/contrast essay structure supports comparing and contrasting two characters, people, themes, vacations, cities, movies, television shows, etc.

To find topics for a compare/contrast essay:

1. Raise questions about the story elements, movies, or whatever you are comparing.

2. Research the questions with a partner.

3. Make a chart of researched data to highlight similarities and differences.

More suggestions for compare/contrast essays

* Share with your partner other historical poems, short stories, and novels.

* Read about historical periods you're interested in on the Internet.

* Find books, stories, and poems about a specific period by Googling the period followed by "young adult literature" (example: Vietnam War, young adult literature).

Finding Topics for Free Choice Writing

With free choice writing, you are in charge of all the stages of writing, and you work independently or with your partner; if necessary, you can get help from your teacher. Learning to manage free choice writing develops your responsibility and independence in completing a writing task. Working independently enables you to apply what you've learned from teachers and writing partners and allows you to demonstrate a greater understanding of the genre you've selected.

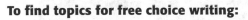

To find topics for free choice writing:

* Skim and reread parts of your writer's notebook.

* Skim the writing in your writing folder.

* Reread mentor texts in your writing folder.

* Talk to your partner about possible topics.

* Write two to three ideas for topics on a piece of notebook paper.

* Share your topics with your teacher to write on a class chart, and then read the class topics list, jotting down any new ideas that come to mind.

* Choose one topic you want to write about—a topic you love and want to work on for a few weeks.

More suggestions for free choice writing

* ❊ Read classmates' free choice writing and find more ideas.

* ❊ Read free choice writing that's been posted on your school's website.

* ❊ Read magazines, such as *Stone Soup,* that feature writing by middle and high school students.

Brainstorming Topics and Ideas

When you brainstorm, you let your mind think about a topic or a problem and share as many ideas as you can.

WHY BRAINSTORM? Brainstorming is a creative thinking tool that artists, managers of corporations, school administrators, people in the military, and heads of governments use to solve problems. Finding ideas for writing is a problem that brainstorming can solve because it encourages a freefall of ideas without judging them. You can choose and evaluate ideas *after* brainstorming.

To refresh your memory of the process, study the brainstormed list on page 22 and notice:

* ❊ Some questions are raised by a partner, and these help to add details to the list.

* ❊ The list contains more ideas than the writer might use for her memoir titled "The Crash."

* ❊ The writer notes at the end of her list that a flashback might be effective.

The Crash

- me in the front seat next to Dave,
- Marge and Jim in the back
- stop at red light
- car behind us crashes into our ~~car~~ Ford
- airbag squishes my body
- Marge crying my head, my head is bleeding
- Dave crying,
- Police come
- Dad helps with report
- No one hurt bad. Just scared.
- Dad drives to emergency room.
- Xray Dave's arm—broken—cast
- Dave's hand dangling from wrist bone
- Dave is 19 driving me and Marge from soccer practice
- Jim came to watch practice— he's in 3rd grade
- called dad so he could help with police—
- man who banged into us okay—
- came to our car to apologize and comfort
- will Dave need operation
- doctors say Dave needs metal plate put in wrist—
- at home we stay with Dave until he falls asleep.
- <u>try a flashback</u>—start with Dave and us in hospital

What kind of car?

How bad was cut on Marge's head?

Why was Dave crying?

Why call dad before 911?

What kind of break for Dave?

How did day end?

Give feelings and thoughts

Where were you going?

Were people in other car okay?

How old was Dave?

Now that you have your topic, it's time to collect related ideas that you can use in your writing. The more ideas you brainstorm, the more choices you have for what to include in your piece. Follow these steps:

1. Talk to your partner about your topic in as much detail as possible.

2. Ask your partner questions that bring up more ideas.

3. Write on notebook paper everything you remember from your talk with your partner. Don't worry about correct spelling or complete sentences. Write words and phrases because you're gathering ideas for writing. Don't stop the flow of ideas—even those quirky ones—by judging them. Just write.

4. Give your brainstormed list to your partner to read.

5. Ask your partner to write on a sticky note any questions about ideas on the list and then return the list and questions to you.

6. Use questions your partner posed to add more ideas to the list and extra details to ideas on the list.

Mining Mentor Texts

A mentor is a teacher. A mentor text is any piece of writing you look at that can teach you or give you an example of writing technique. Mentor texts for different genres can help you understand each genre's structure and learn more about leads, endings, strong verbs, specific nouns, sensory images, etc. What you read on the Internet, in magazines, and in books can teach you about the art of writing well. Everything you read can teach you something new about writing well, from studying how writers foreshadow to understanding the difference between fantasy and science fiction.

FROM READING FOR ENJOYMENT TO READING LIKE A WRITER Here are two ways my students use their independent reading to teach them more about writing that you might want to try:

1. *Jot down words and phrases that speak to you while you read in your writer's notebook.* Some students keep a small pad next to them while they read just to be able to note those words and phrases. Then they reread these words and phrases and use them in their own writing.

2. *Copy a favorite example from your independent reading book*—a poem, a sentence, a lead, an ending, or a technique such as flashback, foreshadowing or sensory images—into your school or online notebook. Writers reread their notebooks to deepen their understanding of a genre and get ideas for their own writing.

Ann Tobias, a book editor, said, "To learn how to write realistic fiction, biography, any genre, read dozens of books in that genre, for these are your best teachers."

Negotiating Criteria

> "I found developing criteria beneficial. Criteria help students shine because they know how to plan and what to revise and edit. Criteria let students' strong points shine and do not penalize them for errors not in the criteria."
>
> **KEATON L., GRADE 7**

Most of the time, teachers use rubrics to grade students' work. Criteria help teachers grade. But criteria also make the writing easier for you, the student, because these guidelines help you plan, draft, revise, and edit. And you may help develop criteria for writing with your classmates and teachers. You may also negotiate the percentage points for each section.

To negotiate criteria:

1. Study a mentor text to figure out content criteria.

2. Work with a partner, the class, and your teacher to negotiate content criteria.

3. Consider the craft and technique criteria that can improve the genre you're working on, such as "Show, don't tell" for narratives and "Vary sentence openings" for essays. Then negotiate these with your teacher, who may also have suggestions.

4. Decide, with your teacher's support, which writing conventions you need to practice.

5. Refer to the criteria when you plan, draft, revise, and edit your writing.

In the boxes on pages 28 and 29 are sample criteria for a short memoir and for an informative essay. Study these to refresh your memory. Use them as resources along with the list headed "Criteria for Diverse Genres" (see your Heinemann website) when developing criteria for free choice and at-school writing.

Criteria for a Short Memoir

Content (45%)

✷ Include a short title that is interesting and relates to the memoir.

✷ Write from the first-person point of view.

✷ Focus on one event and two main people involved.

✷ Use dialogue that reveals characters and moves the plot forward.

Style (craft and technique) (30%)

✷ Create a lead that grabs readers and immediately sets the scene.

✷ Use strong verbs.

Writing conventions (25%)

✷ Mark paragraphs.

✷ Write dialogue correctly.

Criteria for an Informative Essay

Content (60%)

- Audience: Who will read this? How much do they know about the topic?
- Title: Keep it short.
- Introduction: Name the topic and end with a focus statement.
- Body: Write three paragraphs that support the focus statement.
- Ending: Take readers beyond the topic.

Style (craft and technique) (25%)

- Use interesting leads and endings.
- Include a topic sentence for each support paragraph.

Writing conventions (15%)

- Identify and repair faulty pronoun references.
- Punctuate compound and complex sentences correctly.

Creating Writing Plans

A detailed plan makes drafting easy because you've thought through the problem of a story or the supporting details for an essay before drafting. Planning is what all writers—from students to published writers—do. Writing plans differ widely and are often messy because you continually adjust them and add new details. The following suggestions for organizing your ideas into a writing plan that follow can be completed on a computer or on notebook paper.

❖ Create a web.
❖ Use lists.
❖ Design your own graphic organizer.

* Use a storyboard to develop a narrative by drawing pictures with captions. (You'll find a storyboard form on your Heinemann website pages.)

* Take the negotiated criteria and use the content section to create a writing plan.

In the box below is a writing plan for you to review.

Student Writing Plan

Here is Keaton L.'s writing plan for his persuasive essay titled "Do or Don't Have a Soccer Team at School."

Writing Plan for a Persuasive Essay

Name: *Keaton L.*

Directions: *Jot notes for each section.*

Working title: *Do or Don't? (Soccer for School)*

Thesis or position statement: *JWMS should have a soccer team.*

Working lead: *Soccer is an international and popular sport for men and women. My friends and I play it after school, and many of us have joined local travel teams.*

List points and number these from strongest (1) to weakest:

(2) *Many students can be on a team— up to 22 on a team*

(1) *Soccer has variety of positions for every skill type—example of goalie and forward*

(3) *Popular world sport: every country has a team*

(4) *Builds school spirit—gets others going to games and feeling pride*

List two objections to your position and show how you will address each:

(1) *Cost—have fund raisers*

(2) *Other schools don't support having a soccer team—play schools that have teams or play two teams at our school*

Conclusion: How do you think you will end your piece?

Use call to action—get students, coaches, parents, and principal involved

Develop Thesis and Focus Statements for Essays

ANALYTICAL ESSAY

The four-step process in the boxed example on page 34 is a surefire way to create a thesis statement for an analytical essay. Study and review the steps and the example in the box for the topic "growing up." A thesis statement can introduce or lead your essay, or you can end your introduction with the thesis statement.

Forming a Thesis Statement for an Analytical Essay: A Model to Study

Topic: growing up

Steps	Examples
1. Identify the subject.	Making decisions and solving problems can lead to growing up.
2. Turn the subject into a question.	How can making decisions and solving problems lead to growing up?
3. Answer the question with a statement.	When making decisions and solving problems show that an individual is accepting responsibility, that's growing up.
4. Refine the statement into a thesis statement.	Growing up means that an individual can make decisions and accept responsibility for her words and actions.

Now, use the four steps to develop a thesis statement for your analytical essay.

1. Identify your subject.

2. Turn your subject into a question.

3. Answer your question with a statement.

4. Revise your statement into a thesis statement.

Forming a Focus Statement for Informative and Explanatory Essays

A focus statement is the final sentence in an introduction to informative and explanatory essays. A focus statement states the key points and ideas that you will develop in your essay.

You can use this word equation to help you form a clear focus statement:

Narrowed Topic + **Three Key Supporting Details** = **Focus Statement**

You can also follow the five steps listed below:

1. Reread your topic, categories, and notes.
2. Jot what you are trying to show about the topic.
3. Organize what you want to show into a clear focus statement.
4. Have your partner read your focus statement and suggest ways to improve it.
5. Revise your focus statement.

Digging into First Drafts

> "Don't hold back when drafting. First drafts can and do change afterwards."
>
> **MAGGIE G., GRADE 7**

First drafts are messy. You cross out words, phrases, and whole sentences. You draw arrows to reposition a paragraph or sentence. Knowing that all writers' first drafts are messy and imperfect is comforting because it can help you focus on getting it all down on paper.

If you don't already have guidelines for completing a draft for narratives and essays, you can find some on your Heinemann website page.

Following are some reminders that can help you with first drafts:

* Reread your brainstormed list and writing plan several times.

* Put the brainstormed list and writing plan aside when you're writing a narrative because you know the story well. Just let the writing pour out onto the paper. You can revise and edit after drafting.

* Keep the brainstormed list and writing plan close by when you draft an essay so you can refer to them to refresh your memory. Essay arguments and explanations are tougher to recall, so pause and reread parts of your writing plan.

* Let your first draft cool. Put it into your writing folder until the next class. This gives you the distance you need to read your first draft and figure out how to improve it.

* Check your first draft against the content criteria and make adjustments.

Crafting Cool Leads

> "The best leads capture you and make you want to read every word and not put your book down."
> **KEATON L., GRADE 7**

Grab the attention of your audience with the lead and they will keep reading!

To help you with writing tasks you work on at home, I've organized different kinds of leads under each writing genre and included a student example for each one.

First, it's important to review three jobs of a lead:

1. It introduces the topic, sometimes with the help of the title.

2. It grabs the reader's attention.

3. It raises several questions that make the reader want to read more.

Test your lead by noting the questions it raises—questions that compel your readers to read more.

As you review the different types of leads for narrative, argument, and informational writing, you'll see that some types work for all three categories.

> "Try writing several leads until you find the one that works best."
> **MAGGIE G., GRADE 7**

Leads for Narrative Writing

1. Lead with dialogue.

Student example: "Is she purring?" Dad asked as he bent down to look at the cat.

"No," said Anna. "She won't open her eyes. She always opens her eyes and looks at me—but not this morning." Her voice choked with sobs.

2. Lead with a brief story or anecdote.

Student example: I could hear Dad's voice saying, "Be proud of your long hair." But my fourteen-year-old mind hated the pigtails that reached beyond my waist. I raised my mom's sewing shears and cut one pigtail just beneath my right ear.

3. Lead with a quote from a character (story) or person (memoir).

Student example: "Never copy someone else's homework." Mom's words rang inside my head as I used Jeff's geometry homework to copy two proofs.

4. Lead with an action.

Student example: My brother and I jumped up and down, up and down on our parents' new bed. "It's better than a trampoline," Gene shouted. Crash! The mattress caved in, and my brother and I rolled across the bedroom.

5. Lead by setting the scene.

Student example: Small rapids whirled wildly, gaining strength from the river's fast-moving water. Broken tree limbs tossed and leaped out of the water as if they were trout. Wind gusts churned the river as our canoe approached danger.

6. Lead by setting a tone or mood.

Student example: Black clouds eclipsed the afternoon sun, turning day into night. Gentle breezes gathered energy and shook trees, causing leaves and branches to fall. Lightning pierced the dark sky.

7. Lead with a flashback.

Student example: Gramps and I sat by the fire warming our chilled bodies. Why? I wondered. Why did our boat capsize at night?

8. Lead with sensory images.

Student example: As I rang the bell, the beefy smell of pot roast smothered in onions mingled with the hallway air. Tender, juicy meat, I thought. Roasted potatoes. Old iron pot. Jan opened the door, and for a moment I saw my grandma.

9. Lead with sentence fragments.

Student example: Okay, Miranda. He won't call. Won't! I know it for a fact. Never!

Leads for Argument

1. **Include important facts and statistics such as percentages, costs, and results of surveys.** Hard evidence is important when you're trying to persuade others to accept your opinion. You can find hard evidence on the Internet.

   Student example: Local communities need to provide food and clothing for children living in poverty. According to the National Center for Children in Poverty, 15 million children— that's 21% of all children—live in families with incomes below the federal poverty level of $22,050 a year for a family of four.

2. **Quote an authority on your topic.** This can be a student, teacher, parent, doctor, or any expert your reader might respect.

   Student example: Dr. Gregory and Dr. Hilton, both pediatricians, say, "Middle school students need a midmorning snack to have enough energy to concentrate on their schoolwork."

3. **Start with an anecdote.** Use a short, short story to introduce your position and arguments.

   Student example: Imagine you're the only one in the locker room. Everyone else is in the gym. You trip and fall. You can't move because your leg aches. Luckily, your cell phone is handy and you text your mom, who calls the school. Within an hour you're in the emergency room having your leg x-rayed.

4. Include some background information.
Choose details that support your argument and grab the reader's attention.

Student example: Ten years ago our school had a junior marching band, and students rented instruments and took lessons at school. Nonathletic students had an activity they enjoyed, and at the same time, they learned to play an instrument.

Leads for Informative and Explanatory Writing

1. **Lead with a question that doesn't have a yes-or-no answer.**

   Student example: What would you do if a brown bear loped toward you as you picked blueberries and dropped them into a metal bucket?

2. **Lead with an interesting or fascinating fact.**

   Student example: Because owls have eyes that point forward, like human eyes, they can watch an object with both eyes.

3. **Lead with a thought-provoking quote.**

   Student example: "Rain forests supply 20% of the planet's fresh water supply."

4. **Lead with sensory images.**

   Student example: Rotten eggs, I thought. My nose twitched and I knew that my brother was at it again.

5. **Lead by setting the scene.**

   Student example: Silently, mist crept across the open meadow. Weighted with dewdrops, the white veil masked the green grass.

6. **Lead with an anecdote.**

   Student example: The copperhead reared its head. Frozen, I stared at it. Run! Run fast! the voice in my head shouted. But the snake struck before I could flee.

Seeking Satisfying Endings

> "The ideal ending leaves a reader wanting more—wishing the story wasn't over."
>
> **KEATON L., GRADE 7**

Endings for Narrative and Informative/Explanatory Writing

You can end narratives, essays, directions, and articles that inform and/or explain information using one of the techniques for leads. In addition, the questions below, which you can ask yourself or discuss with a partner, will help you decide on the just-right place to end your writing:

* ❊ Do you think the ending is effective?

* ❊ If yes, how does it connect to the big purpose of the piece? What makes it satisfying?

* ❊ If no, what makes it unsatisfying? Did you try techniques for your ending that were similar to those for leads?

* ❊ Why did you choose to end the piece at this point?

Endings for Argument

The three kinds of endings that follow are powerful with forms of persuasive writing:

1. **Call the reader to action.** A call to action suggests specific ways for others to make change happen.

   Student example: If you believe that a healthy midmorning snack can give you the energy and focus to learn more, then write to the principal, the head of your school board, parents, and teachers.

2. **Make a logical prediction.** A logical prediction uses the arguments in your writing to show the future benefits of your position or the bad consequences of ignoring your argument.

   Student example: Having your cell phone handy lets you contact a family member in an emergency and can get the help an injured or sick student needs.

3. **Pose a thought-provoking question.** Questions can get readers thinking about your arguments on a position.

   Student example: Do you want students to concentrate on their growling stomachs or on your subject?

"When I'm writing a story, I have trouble with endings. If I change ideas in the story, then I have to change the ending to match it."
MAGGIE G., GRADE 7

Revising for Craft and Technique

Engineers, architects, surgeons, and dentists don't have revision options; they need to get it right the first time. With writers, it's different because writers can rework and improve the craft and technique in their writing until they get it right.

The criteria you and classmates negotiate for a genre will let you know which craft and technique lessons to review before plunging into revising your writing. In the list below, you'll find five basic beneficial strategies that will help you improve your writing when revising for any craft element or technique:

1. Give your writing a rest for a day or two.

2. Read your writing out loud.

3. Turn to criteria to self-evaluate an early draft.

4. Rewrite parts related to content, style, and craft criteria.

5. Ask your partner for feedback.

Here are five craft and technique lessons that can make almost any piece sparkle.

1. Show a Character's or Person's Personality Traits

This technique is critical for narrative fiction and memoir but can also be useful if you have an anecdote anywhere in an essay. Almost all the tips in "Writing Techniques for Showing Personality Traits" were used in this Sample Dialogue.

Sample Dialogue

"Watch out for those rapids!" Jim shouted.

"Can't control this raft!" hollered Dave over the roar of the water.

"Bail out," ordered Jim.

"No way!" screamed Dave as he closed his eyes and prayed.

Writing techniques for showing personality traits

❉ Use dialogue and choose words that reveal personality traits.

In the sample: "Watch out" and "Bail out" reveal Jim's personality. He's used to giving orders.

❉ Include speaker tags because these show the emotional state of the character or person and the tone of voice.

In the sample: Speaker tags such as "shouted" and "hollered" offer insights into each boy's emotional state.

❉ Show the character's or person's inner thoughts during a dialogue, during a conflict, or in another setting.

In the sample: The word "prayed" reveals how anxious Dave felt.

❉ Include a character's or person's decisions and actions.

In the sample: Dave decides to stay with his raft, showing that he's determined and courageous.

❉ Present how other characters or people see a specific character or person.

❉ Let readers see how a character or person deals with an event or a problem.

In the sample: Jim shouts to warn Dave of the danger.

✳ Provide the physical reactions of the character or person.

In the sample: The phrase "closed his eyes and prayed" offers insights into both the situation and Dave's personality.

More uses of dialogue
You can use dialogue, inner thoughts, and what others say to show time passing, to mention and describe a setting, and to give the reader important background information.

2. Use Strong Verbs to Build Powerful Images

Consider the following steps to strengthen the verbs in everything you write:

1. Study and discuss the strong verbs in a mentor text like "Funeral" by Ralph Fletcher.

2. Circle four to five verbs in your writing that need strengthening; ask your partner or teacher to help you identify verbs if you have difficulty with this step.

3. Discuss possible alternative verbs with your partner.

4. Brainstorm in the margin or on a sticky note some alternative verbs.

5. Choose the verb that best fits the context of your writing and creates strong imagery.

Finding Strong Verbs

Example: Danny <u>went</u> to the store.

Alternate choices: jogged, biked, hitchhiked, skated

Revision: Danny <u>biked</u> to the store.

3. Show, Don't Tell

Professional writers rate "Show, don't tell" as an extremely important technique for all kinds of writing. The more you study mentor texts and the more you write, the better you will know when it's fine to tell and when it's best to show. Showing offers readers the details to infer whether the ocean is calm, the dog is vicious, or the tree is pretty. Revising to show rather than tell can improve any piece. Here's how:

1. Find a telling sentence in your writing to change to a showing sentence.

2. Complete a short brainstormed list of details to include in your showing rewrite.

3. Rewrite the telling sentence using some or all of the details you brainstormed.

4. Complete your rewrite in one to two sentences.

From Telling to Showing

Telling sentence: The <u>tree</u> is <u>pretty</u>.

Brainstormed list: maple, meadow, alone, leaves gold, crimson, orange

Showing sentence: The <u>lone maple</u> stands tall surveying the meadow, its <u>shimmering crimson and gold leaves</u> gently falling to the ground.

4. Use Specific Nouns

A general noun, such as *things,* does not create the visual images that specific nouns like *fishing pole and reel, tackle box,* and *spoon hooks* paint in readers' minds. Here are some ways to revise for specific nouns:

- Study and discuss passages rich in specific nouns from different mentor texts.
- Work with a partner to rewrite sentences with general nouns, changing these to specific nouns.
- Circle four to five general nouns in your writing that need to be specific; ask your partner or teacher to help you identify some general nouns if you have difficulty.
- Discuss possible alternative specific nouns with your partner.
- Brainstorm in the margin or on a sticky note alternative specific nouns.
- Choose the specific nouns that fit the context of your writing to create strong imagery.

General nouns: The dance planners brought <u>stuff</u> for the <u>dance</u> to school.

Specific nouns for "stuff": red balloons, candy hearts, pretzels, potato chips

Specific kind of dance: Valentine's Day dance

Revision: For the <u>Valentine's Day Dance</u> at school, the planning team brought <u>red balloons, red lanterns and streamers, candy hearts, pretzels, and soda</u>.

5. Add Figurative Language

A simile, a metaphor, personification, and onomatopoeia can help you create in readers' minds both pictures and sensory images of scenes, events, characters, and people. Refresh your memory of these writing tools by reading and thinking about the definitions and student examples in the box that follows.

Figurative Language: Writers' Tools

Simile: a comparison of two unlike things that have one thing in common; uses *like* or *as.*

Student example: She hissed <u>like</u> a snake ready to strike.

Metaphor: an implied comparison of two unlike things that have one thing in common without using *like* or *as*; often equates the two things using *is, was, are,* or *were.*

Student example: The grass <u>is</u> Earth's comforter.

Personification: a technique that gives human traits and feelings to something that isn't human.

Student example: The <u>river swallowed</u> chairs and tables as it flooded its banks.

Onomatopoeia: a technique that uses words that sound like what they name.

Student example: The <u>crunch-crunch</u> of children <u>marching</u> across the snowy meadow drowned the sound of cars in the distance.

Editing for Writing Conventions

It's tough for you to spot errors in punctuation, wrong pronoun references, missing transitions between paragraphs, etc. As a writer reads, her brain corrects her errors so she doesn't even notice them. Your writing partner can really help editing for writing conventions because he is unfamiliar or less familiar with the piece and can spot errors and omissions.

The criteria you and your classmates negotiate for a genre will let you know which writing convention lessons to review before asking your partners to help with editing. In the list below, you'll find five basic beneficial strategies for editing for writing conventions:

1. Edit for one writing convention at a time. This means rereading the piece a few times.

2. Read the writing out loud and think about the writing convention you're editing. To slow down the reading, point a pencil under each word.

3. Seek help from your teacher when you and your partner disagree.

4. Edit for usage and punctuation. Sometimes this means marking paragraphs or adding commas;

other times you will rewrite to repair a run-on sentence or vary a sentence opening.

5. Add sentences to create transitions between paragraphs, or use prepositional phrases to add details.

Here are nine conventions that are often tricky for writers.

1. Writing Dialogue

If you don't already have a tip sheet for writing dialogue, download it from your Heinemann website: www.smartwritinghandbook.com

Revision tips for direct quotations

1. Read your story and pinpoint words such as *said, answered, questioned, wondered, thought.* These words tell you if someone is speaking or thinking.

2. Find the speaker's words and place quotation marks over the first and last words spoken.

3. Check to make sure the first word of the direct quotation starts with a capital letter.

4. Insert punctuation—a period (.), comma (,), question mark (?), or exclamation point (!)—before the closing quotation marks.

5. Look for words such as *wondered, thought, told himself* as these usually indicate inner thoughts. Don't use quotation marks with inner thoughts.

6. Study the examples in the box; these illustrate how to punctuate direct quotations and inner thoughts.

Punctuating Direct Quotations and Inner Thoughts

Here are examples of punctuation for direct quotations and inner thoughts. Note the commas, periods, and other end punctuation (?!) and where the quotation marks go. Note, too, that inner thoughts do not use quotation marks. Important punctuation is underlined to call your attention to it in these examples:

"Clean up your room now," ordered Mom.

Polly asked, "Can you go shopping with me tomorrow?"

"We lost the volleyball game," Coach Brown said, "but I'm proud of the team's sportsmanship!"

"The movie projector broke," said Tanya. "We cruised the mall to pass the time."

I hope we have pizza for dinner, thought Jenny.

2. Paragraphing a Narrative

Your first-draft writing goal is to get that story onto paper. Chances are you're not thinking about separating paragraphs at this stage; it's the story, the plot, that's unfolding. Once you have a draft, reread it and use the symbol for paragraph (¶) to mark where you should start a new paragraph. But how do you know where to put it?

TIPS FOR MARKING PARAGRAPHS IN NARRATIVES

Start a new paragraph when:

- ✳ the speaker in a dialogue changes.
- ✳ the setting or the place changes.
- ✳ the situation changes.
- ✳ inner thoughts reveal feelings.
- ✳ the time changes.

3. Paragraphing a Persuasive Essay

Most likely, you're not thinking about separating paragraphs while writing a first draft. Once you have a draft, reread it and mark the places where you need a new paragraph with a paragraph symbol(¶). Use the guidelines that follow to paragraph your essay.

Guidelines for paragraphing a persuasive essay
Reread your first draft out loud and use the paragraph symbol (¶) to mark paragraphs. You'll need separate paragraphs for these elements of a persuasive essay:

* Lead or introduction
* Ending
* Arguments for your opinion
* Arguments against your opinion

Note: If you have four or more arguments stating your opinion, you might need two paragraphs.

4. Writing Transition Sentences Between Paragraphs

Writing a sentence or two to make one paragraph lead to the next is a challenge for all writers. Rereading first drafts to make sure there are smooth transitions between paragraphs and pinpointing places that need a transition are the first steps. You can use the list of questions and tips on the next page to test your draft for transition sentences between paragraphs.

QUESTIONS AND TIPS FOR EVALUATING TRANSITIONS BETWEEN PARAGRAPHS

Questions

* ❊ Is there a transition sentence?
* ❊ Does the transition sentence smooth the way to the topic of the next paragraph?
* ❊ Do you know the topic of the paragraph that you are transitioning to?

Tips

* ❊ Use a statement to transition.
* ❊ Use a question to transition.
* ❊ Use words and phrases to introduce transition sentences: *however, moreover, therefore, in addition, most often.*

To review paragraphing and transitions in a persuasive essay, read the mentor text on the Heinemann website.

5. Varying Sentence Openings

Often, when reading a first draft, you or your writing partner will notice that some sentences that follow one another start the same way. This is not unusual in a first draft where you're working hard to transfer a story or information from your mind to paper. That's why it's helpful to have some ideas to vary sentence openings in your writing. In the following box is a list of words and some tips that can help you rewrite sentences that start the same way.

WORDS AND TIPS FOR VARYING SENTENCE OPENINGS

Words

meanwhile	until	whoever	unless
as soon as	whatever	since	because
when	if	what	while
immediately	afterward	now	later
instead of	although	wherever	both

Tips

1. Circle a repeated word and any ideas repeated within the sentences.
2. Combine sentences with related ideas.
3. Eliminate repeated ideas within sentences.
4. Add or delete words to make the writing and ideas clear.

Revising Sentence Openings

Here's an example of how a sixth grader used words from the list on page 62 to vary the openings of three sentences that began almost the same way. Remember that there is more than one way to revise these sentences.

Original sentences

Tension invaded the locker room. Sixth grade boys near my locker stopped changing for gym and stared at me. The tension made shivers go up my spine when I opened my locker. The tension escalated and sweat poured down my face and back when I read the note: *Sissies need to grow up. We'll make that happen.*

Student's rewrite

As soon as I walked into the locker room, sixth grade boys near my locker stopped changing for gym and stared at me. Tension, thick as dense fog, sent shivers up my spine as I opened my locker. Immediately, I saw the note. Beads of sweat formed on my face and back after I read it: *Sissies need to grow up. We'll make that happen.*

6. Identifying and Repairing Run-Ons

Most students have run-on sentences in their first drafts. It's easy to edit those run-ons and improve the clarity of your writing. The first type of run-on is tough to identify because both sentences seem connected.

Example: Josh and Maria bought a pizza they ate half before arriving home.

The sentences seem connected because "they" refers to Josh and Maria. However, there are two separate sentences here, and each has a subject and a verb:

❋ Josh and Maria bought a pizza.

❋ They ate half before arriving home.

There are four ways to repair this sentence:

1. Create two separate sentences.

Example: Josh and Maria bought a pizza. They ate half before arriving home.

2. Use a conjunction and a comma.

Example: Josh and Maria bought a pizza, and they ate half before arriving home.

3. Remove the subject "they" from the second sentence.

Example: Josh and Maria bought a pizza and ate half before arriving home.

4. Use a semicolon to separate each complete sentence.

Example: Josh and Maria bought a pizza; they ate half before arriving home.

The second type of run-on sentence has several ideas connected with words such as *and, and then, then.* Test for this type of run-on by looking for sentences that go on for three or more lines.

Example: Mike and Jose rented the canoe and then went down to the dock and picked a red one and made sure there were two paddles, then they bought some sandwiches and soda at a store and put on life jackets and went out on the river.

There are many ways to rewrite this run-on sentence. Be prepared to add or delete words and change the order of events.

Revision: Mike and Jose rented a red canoe. At the dock they checked the canoe to make sure there were two paddles. After they put on life jackets, both boys bought sandwiches and soda at the dock store for the trip down the river.

Tips for editing a run-on with several ideas

1. Rearrange sentences that are too long and contain ideas that don't relate.

2. Add or delete words or phrases as you edit.

3. Create two sentences out of one that changes places, ideas, or time.

4. Reread your rewrite out loud to see if it makes sense.

7. Identifying and Repairing Faulty Pronoun References

There's really only one simple rule for pronoun references: a pronoun must match its antecedent in gender and number. But what does that mean? It's helpful to understand the terms!

Pronoun. A word that replaces a noun—*he, him, himself, it, them, their, that, those,* etc.

Antecedent. The word a pronoun refers to in a sentence. *Example:* Rachel plays tennis for her school, and she has won every game. Here, "she" refers to Rachel, so Rachel is the antecedent of "she."

Gender. Male (*he, him*) female (*she, her*), or neutral (*it*).

Number. Singular (one) or plural (two or more).

Often, students refer to a singular noun with a plural pronoun or to a plural noun with a singular pronoun. Using a four-column chart can help you test for and correct faulty pronoun references. The box shows how a chart can help you spot a faulty pronoun reference.

Faulty Pronoun References

Sentence: The dress was too expensive for Sally, so they shopped in a different store.

Here's how the four-column chart helps to identify the faulty pronoun reference.

Pronoun	Antecedent	Gender	Singular or Plural
They	Sally	Female	plural pronoun, singular antecedent

The rewrite can change either the pronoun or the antecedent.

Rewrites: The dress was too expensive for <u>Sally</u>, so <u>she</u> shopped in a different store.

The dress was too expensive for <u>Sally and her mom</u>, so <u>they</u> shopped in a different store.

8. Punctuating Complex Sentences

A complex sentence contains an independent clause and a dependent clause.

Independent clause. A complete sentence with a subject and verb.

Example: Maria won first prize at the county fair for baking a great apple pie.

Dependent clause. The common type of dependent clause starts with a subordinating conjunction, and even though this clause has a subject and a verb, it is not a complete sentence.

Example: Although she had never baked before

Subordinating conjunctions. Words such as *when, if,* and *because* that introduce a group of words with a subject and verb called a dependent clause. When the dependent clause starts a sentence, it is set off with a comma; no comma is needed if the dependent clause comes after the independent clause.

Examples: Although she had never baked before, Maria won first prize at the county fair for baking a great apple pie.

Maria won first prize at the county fair for baking a great apple pie although she had never baked before.

Commas with Dependent Clauses

Subordinating conjunctions: after, although, as, as if, as long as, as soon as, as though, because, before, if, in order that, provided that, since, so, so that, that, though, till, unless, until, when, where, whereas, while

Examples of complex sentences:

Because Bobby trained for six months, he won the nationals for distance running.

Bobby won the nationals for distance running because he trained for six months.

9. Using Prepositional Phrases

You can use prepositional phrases to add specific details
to sentences as well as to vary sentence openings. Use
the chart that follows, with its list of prepositions, as
a resource and a memory refresher when you create
prepositional phrases to revise sentence openings (see the
tips on page 62) and to add specific details to sentences.

Prepositional Phrases				
across	behind	in	over	up
amid	below	into	since	upon
after	by	near	throughout	with
against	down	off	to	without
at	during	on	toward	
around	for	onto	under	

Prepositions introduce a group of words called a
prepositional phrase. A prepositional phrase can end in a
noun or a pronoun. This ending word is called the *object of
the preposition.*

Examples using pronouns: for <u>him</u>; with <u>them</u>

Grammar fact: Pronouns that end prepositional phrases are
the object form of personal pronouns (*me, you, him, her, it,
us, you, them*).

Examples using nouns: under the <u>starry sky</u>; without <u>Robert</u>

Grammar fact: Nouns that end prepositional phrases can
be common or proper nouns.

Questions Help Writers Add Details to Sentences Using Prepositional Phrases

To test whether a sentence would benefit from extra details, you can ask questions that start with these words:

where, what, who, when, why, how

The example that follows shows you how helpful questions can be. I've underlined the prepositional phrases that add details and imagery.

Sample sentence: Mom visited Grandma.

Where does Grandma live?

What made Mom visit?

Who else visited Grandma? *or* Who came with Mom?

When did the visit occur?

Why did Mom visit?

How long was the visit?

Rewrite that uses specific details (underlined) based on the questions:

Shortly after Grandma called our house around 2 A.M. on Monday morning, Mom and Dad drove for three hours to visit Grandma in her home in Falls Church, Virginia. A fall resulting in a twisted ankle kept Grandma in her chair, so Mom and Dad planned to take her back to our house for rest and care.

A Crash Course
on Commas

Commas can flummox writers because commas are frequently optional. Yet leaving out some commas can confuse readers like the title of that well-known grammar book, *Eats Shoots & Leaves*. *Eats Shoots & Leaves* might describe a panda feeding on bamboo, but add two commas and see how the meaning changes: *Eats, Shoots, & Leaves* now might describe a shoot 'em up cowboy in a saloon.

Many writers were taught to read a draft out loud and place a comma after a pause. Believe me, this can result in too many commas and rereading a passage out loud too many times to check for pauses. Not a good use of your time. Instead, I'm listing some comma rules along with examples that can bring clarity to your writing. I won't cover the following rules for commas because they are already covered in this handbook:

- ❋ Commas and writing correct dialogue (see pages 57–58)

- ❋ Commas and repairing run-on sentences (see pages 64–65)

- ❋ Commas and creating complex sentences (see pages 68–69)

Commas and words in a series

Place a comma after each word in a series. Being an English teacher, I favor always placing a comma before the conjunction because it creates clarity.

Example: Helena packed her ballet shoes, warm-up leggings, and black leotard.

Commas and coordinate adjectives

Separate adjectives with commas if they pass these two tests:

1. Switch the adjectives' order and the sentence still makes sense.

2. Place "and" between the adjectives and the sentence still makes sense.

Example: Mittens is a soft fluffy kitten.

Test 1: Mittens is a fluffy soft kitten.

Test 2: Mittens is a soft and fluffy kitten.

Result: Mittens is a soft, fluffy kitten.

Commas and cumulative adjectives

Cumulative adjectives build on one another and don't need a comma between them. The order of the adjectives does matter, and changing the order changes the meaning and/or the writer's intention.

Example: Dad ate sizzling, succulent steak and crispy, crunchy fried potatoes.

Commas and adjectives ending in *-ly*

When a series or a list of adjectives includes an adjective that ends in *-ly,* set the adjectives off with commas.

Example: Marina takes a long, challenging, daily jog through her neighborhood.

Commas and coordinating conjunctions

Use a comma and a coordinating conjunction to separate two complete sentences, each with its own subject and verb.

Examples:

1. Jose purchased three cartons of sodas, and he delivered them to the gym for tonight's dance. (subjects and verbs: "Jose purchased" and "he delivered")

2. Margo trained all month for the cross-country race, but Sheila won the race. (subjects and verbs: "Margo trained" and "Sheila won")

3. The gash on his head needed stitches, so Josh hurried to the Emergency Room. (subjects and verbs: "gash...needed" and "Josh hurried")

Commas and *if* clauses

A conditional sentence describes a possible condition and its consequences. Use a comma to set off the condition (*if* clause) from the consequence.

Example: If you don't clean your room by noon, you won't go to the movies today.

Commas and nonessential elements

Use commas to set off a nonessential element, such as an appositive, from the main sentence. *Appositive* is a term for extra information in the sentence. Here's the question you need to answer when considering commas: Is the appositive nonessential or extra information that could be deleted without changing the meaning of the sentence? If it's nonessential or extra, use commas; if it's essential (not extra), do not use commas.

Example of essential appositive (no commas): Head coach Maria accepted the trophy for her undefeated team.

Example of nonessential appositive (with commas): Maria, the head coach, accepted the trophy for her undefeated team.

Commas and direct address

Set off the name or title of a person being directly talked to with commas.

Examples:

1. Sandi, please pick up the papers under your desk.
2. Please pick up the papers under your desk, Sandi.
3. Please, Sandi, pick up the papers under your desk.
4. Doctor, please see this man next.
5. Please see this man next, Doctor.
6. Please, Doctor, see this man next.

Commas and interjections

After an interjection at the beginning of a sentence:

Use a comma when the meaning is not dramatic.
Example: Gosh, that pool seems deep.

Use a period to show finality.
Example: Nope. I'm not jumping off the high diving board.

Use an exclamation point to show strong feeling.
Example: Wow! That storm ripped the tree out of the ground!

Review of some common comma rules

Writing dates: It happened on Tuesday, September 20, 2011.

Writing cities and states: Janet's vacation was in Tucson, Arizona.

Writing numbers over 999: He counted 1,021 pennies.

Writing greetings and closings in letters:

Dear Murray,

Sincerely, Mrs. Robb

Final Note

Keep this handbook close by whether you're working on school assignments or writing to discover your feelings about peer pressure, friendships, trust, and growing up. Use the tips and examples both to communicate your personal vision to others and to explore your own feelings, attitudes, and behaviors. As I said at the beginning, this handbook is for you! Use it to learn more about the writing process and to improve your writing. I know you can make this happen!

Index